Early 1900s

Governments pass laws controlling nurse registration.

1854-1860

Florence Nightingale reforms nursing in British army hospitals and sets up a pioneer nurse training school.

1914-1918 and 1939-1945

Thousands of nurses care for troops in two world wars. They win great respect and admiration.

1909

The United States' first university degree course in nursing is offered, in Minnesota.

1861-1865

Untrained women volunteer as nurses on both sides in the Civil War.

2015

There are over 20 million trained nurses working worldwide. At least 75 percent are women.

The Nightingale Pledge

In 1893, in Detroit, Michigan, pioneer nurse educator Lystra Gretter suggested that newly trained nurses should make a solemn promise to uphold the highest possible standards of nursing care. Gretter called this promise "The Nightingale Pledge," in honor of Florence Nightingale. Many nurses around the world still make a similar promise at their graduation ceremonies today.

Here is Gretter's Nightingale Pledge, in modern words:

"In front of God and all the people gathered here today I promise to live honestly and decently, and faithfully to practice my profession as a nurse.

"I will not do anything wicked or hurtful to myself or to others, and I will not give patients any harmful medicines.

"I will do all I can to uphold and improve high standards of nursing care. I will keep all information about my patients and their families strictly confidential.

"I will work loyally in a team with all other health-care professionals. It is my mission to bring health, and so I dedicate myself to working devotedly for human welfare."

Florence Nightingale is also honored every year on International Nurses Day. It is celebrated worldwide on May 12. Why was that date chosen? It was Florence Nightingale's birthday!

Author:

Fiona Macdonald studied history at
Cambridge University, England, and at the
University of East Anglia. She has taught in
schools, universities, and in adult education, and
is the author of numerous books for children on
historical topics.

Artist:

David Antram was born in Brighton, England,
in 1958. He studied at Eastbourne College of Art
and then worked in advertising for 15 years before
becoming a full-time artist. He has illustrated many
children's nonfiction books.

Series creator:

David Salariya was born in Dundee,
Scotland. He has illustrated a wide range of books
and has created and designed many new series
for publishers in the UK and overseas. David
established The Salariya Book Company in 1989.
He lives in Brighton, England, with his wife,
illustrator Shirley Willis, and their son, Jonathan.

Editor: **Jacqueline Ford**

Editorial Assistant: **Mark Williams**

Published in Great Britain in 2017 by
The Salariya Book Company Ltd
25 Marlborough Place, Brighton BN1 1UB

ISBN-13: 978-0-531-22462-5 (lib. bdg.) 978-0-531-22491-5 (pbk.)

All rights reserved.
Published in 2017 in the United States
by Franklin Watts
An imprint of Scholastic Inc.

A CIP catalog record for this book is available
from the Library of Congress.

Printed and bound in China.
Printed on paper from sustainable sources.

1 2 3 4 5 6 7 8 9 10 R 26 25 24 23 22 21 20 19 18 17

Very important!

The text and pictures in this book
are for interest and information
only. THEY ARE NOT MEDICAL
ADVICE. If you are worried about
your health, you should see a doctor,
nurse, or other health professional.

You Wouldn't Want to Live Without™

Nurses!

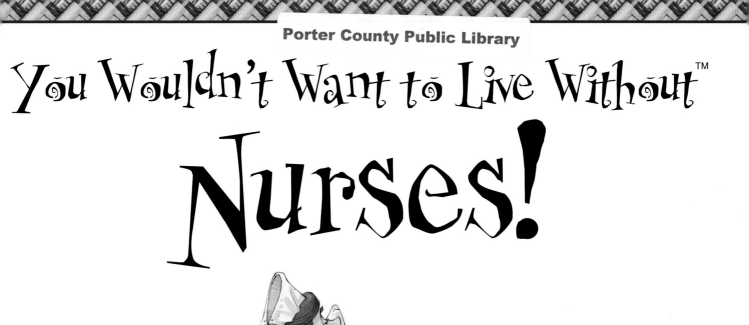

Written by
Fiona Macdonald

Illustrated by
David Antram

Series created by
David Salariya

Franklin Watts®
An Imprint of Scholastic Inc.

Contents

Introduction

Usually you're healthy and full of energy. But just the other day, you had a bad accident. You fell off your bike, bumped your head, and broke your arm and your leg! Now you're in the hospital, but you're getting better quickly and will soon go home. As you lie in your hospital bed, you think about the nurses who are taking care of you. They are so kind, so patient, so caring. They've done so much to help you. Imagine if you didn't have someone to care for you when you were sick. Nurses do such an important job around the world, and help so many people to feel better every day. You really wouldn't want to live without nurses!

Call the Nurse!

Have you ever gotten sick at school, or fallen down and hurt yourself while playing? Then the school nurse probably took care of you. She cleaned your cuts, checked that no bones were broken, and said a few kind words to comfort you. Like all other nurses around the world, your school nurse has been trained to examine her patients, assess (judge) their medical needs, and provide the correct advice or treatment. Every day, school nurses help students in so many different ways.

LICE AREN'T NICE!
Lice feed on human blood and their bites are itchy. Nurses search hair so that lice can be found, removed, and stopped from spreading to and infecting other people.

ONWARD AND UPWARD.
School nurses keep careful records of your height and weight to check that you are growing in a healthy way.

Don't worry, we'll have you fixed up in no time!

Top Tip

The school nurse can also teach you how to care for your teeth so that they stay clean, healthy, and strong. Remember to brush your teeth at least twice a day, and always at bedtime.

EAT WELL, STAY WELL.
Good food helps bodies grow and minds develop. The school nurse can tell you what's best to eat to help you reach your full potential.

DAILY DOSE.
If you have a health condition and have to take pills or use an inhaler, the school nurse can help you make sure that you're getting the right amount of medicine.

A Caring Career

A school nurse is just one kind of nursing professional. There are many, many others. Today, nurses can choose to train for over 200 specialties. But wherever nurses work and whatever nurses do, they all have one thing in common: They have made caring their career. Caring is not only being kind—although it includes that, of course. Nurses also need patience, toughness, cheerfulness, a real interest in other people, and a willingness to deal with messy, yucky tasks.

The Six "C"s

Nurses often say that they need six special personal qualities to do their job well. Each one begins with the letter C. The best nurses have them all!

Care

Compassion

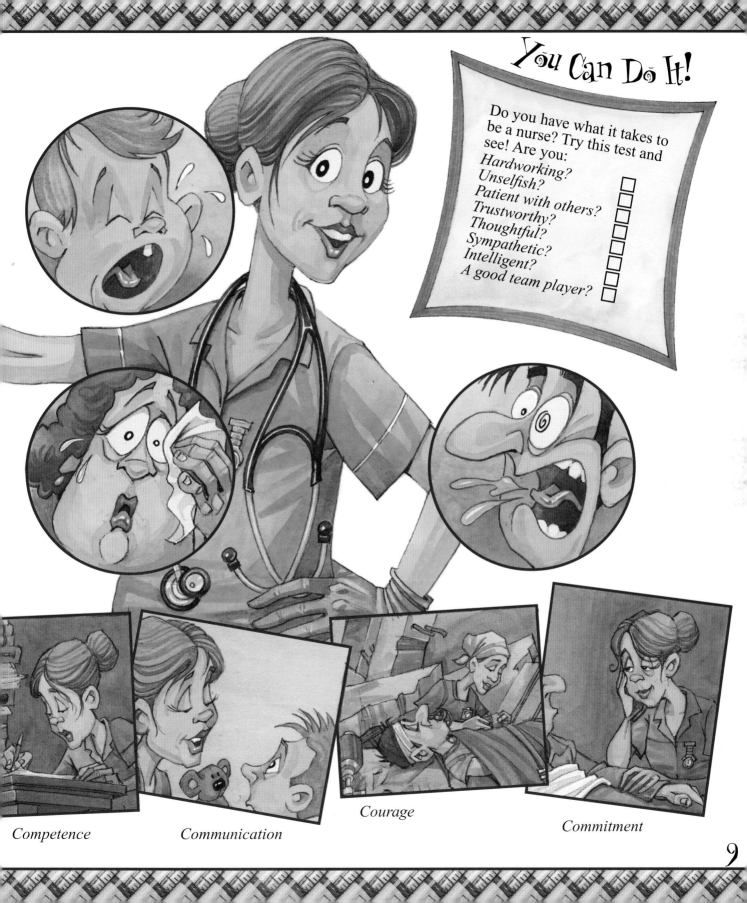

Do you have what it takes to be a nurse? Try this test and see! Are you:

Hardworking?

Unselfish?

Patient with others?

Trustworthy?

Thoughtful?

Sympathetic?

Intelligent?

A good team player?

Competence

Communication

Courage

Commitment

9

Nursed at Home

Nowadays, we expect trained nurses to take care of us when we get sick. However, until recently, most people had to manage without professional nursing care. For thousands of years, mothers, wives, and daughters cared for sick loved ones at home. In the past, people thought that caregiving was a natural female instinct, as well as a woman's duty. But of course not all women were born with nursing skills! Until the 19th century, most family caregivers had no training, but relied on advice from older, more experienced, women. That could sometimes be dangerous!

SICK IN BED? Until around 1800, the local wise woman might have offered you one of her home remedies made from herbs—perhaps with added magic!

WORTH THE MONEY? Until the 20th century, if you were old or sick but wealthy, you likely hired a private nurse. She'd have been pleasant and polite, but not have known much about medicine.

POOR, HOME ALONE, and needing care? Before around 1850, a cheap nurse would have watched by your bedside—but might have been dirty, lazy, and gossipy.

EXPECTING A BABY? From around 600 BCE, you could hire a fashionable new man midwife. He would have had more training than a woman, but less experience.

In the past, in remote areas, there might have been no doctors or nurses for hundreds of miles. So people kept medicine chests stocked with remedies for common illnesses.

I told you not to eat so much!

A MOTHER'S CARE. Our modern word "nurse" comes from the Latin word *nutrix*, which is over 2,000 years old. It means "person who feeds babies and cares for them"—like a human or animal mother.

Care Not Cure

Today, we admire doctors and nurses as heroes who fight disease, heal injuries, and save lives. But in the past, before modern medical advances, many illnesses could not be cured, and nurses or family caregivers had to take care of people who would never get better. If a doctor said there was no hope, it was still a caregiver's job to keep their patient clean, warm, fed, and free from pain—and to help them go to the bathroom. Some caregivers offered spiritual comfort, too, by reading holy books to patients, and saying prayers with them.

The Good Samaritan

In Christian countries, the Bible story of the Good Samaritan was very popular. It told how a stranger cared for a badly injured man, even though he came from a different community. It contained a powerful message: We should all help people in trouble, whoever they may be.

Attacked...

...left to die...

...robbed!

Oh no! The doctor can't cure him!

A stranger approaches...

...helps the poor victim...

...takes him to safety...

...and pays for his care.

Houses of Healing

Today, if we are really sick, we go to the hospital. But in the past, there were not many hospitals—and they were not healthy places to be. Until around 1850, most hospitals were run by charities or religious organizations. They were often crowded, and they were always smelly and full of germs (bacteria and viruses). Sick people were sent there to keep them away from healthy people. Or they went to the hospital to die, if there was no one to care for them at home.

STAY AWAY. In the Middle Ages, to avoid catching diseases, people would send a sick person to a "pest house," far out of town.

MAGIC OR MEDICINE? In ancient Egypt or Greece, sick people could go to a temple, where priests would ask the gods to cure them. The priests might also try to heal someone with medicines, simple surgery, or magic amulets, like the Eye of Horus, below. Their male servants helped them, like nurses.

COULD YOU GIVE CARE in these conditions? In busy, crowded church hospitals, nuns did their best to nurse dying patients—and they helped to prepare dead bodies for burial, too.

Ancient Egyptian priests mixed some very strange medicines.

•Eye trouble? Use fried ox liver or powdered juniper twigs.
•Stomachache? Have some cumin, goose fat, and milk.
•Losing your hair? Try fat from lion, hippo, crocodile, and goose.

15

The New Nurses

Nowadays, we know that germs cause disease, and that keeping clean is an important part of staying healthy. But until around 1850, nobody understood why dirt could be dangerous. Doctors and nurses often wore dirty clothes, and visitors described horrific conditions in hospitals. Not only were the hospitals filthy, they also lacked good food, clean water, soap, bandages, medicines, and proper nursing care. There was a public outcry that "something must be done!" Brave, determined reformers took up the challenge, training new, professional nurses and keeping hospitals superclean.

Look, listen, and learn!

THE LADY WITH THE LAMP. That's what they called Florence Nightingale (1820–1910). In 1854, she was sent to a British army hospital in Turkey to treat British soldiers of the Crimean War. Appalled by the dirt (and rats!) she worked tirelessly to improve cleanliness and patient care. In 1860, she set up the world's first nonreligious nurse training school. Her work made her a national heroine, and created a new public respect for trained, skilled nurses.

TO TRAIN TO BE a new nurse, you'd learn anatomy (body structure) and physiology (how the body works), and about medicines, hygiene, and hospital routine.

How It Works

Beginning in 1903 (in the U.S.) and 1919 (in the UK), nurses had to be properly trained and registered with nursing associations. Before those dates, almost anyone could call themselves a nurse.

Clara Barton (1821–1912)

Dorothea Dix (1802–1887)

BATTLEFIELD ANGELS. Around 5,000 untrained women volunteered to care for wounded soldiers during the Civil War (1851–1865). They were led by Clara Barton (who also founded the American Red Cross) and health-care campaigner and prison reformer Dorothea Dix. Leaders and volunteers bravely did their best, but the war showed that the U.S. urgently needed trained nurses. The first U.S. nurse training school opened in New York City in 1871.

Observation and Communication

In addition to keeping us clean and comfortable, nurses listen to our worries and explain our medical treatments to us in ways we can understand. They sympathize with grieving family members when patients die, and speak up for patients who are unable to put their thoughts and feelings into words. Doctors also rely on nurses to observe patients' vital signs, such as temperature, breathing, and heart rate, and keep accurate records of them. That is a big responsibility!

HEALING HANDS. A nurse's gentle touch will soothe you, but she's also feeling for signs of illness, such as clamminess or shivering.

TOO HOT? TOO COLD? The nurse will take your temperature. If it's too high, too low, or keeps changing, that could be a sign of sickness.

He's getting better! Do you want to tell him, or shall I?

BREATHE IN... AND OUT ... Are you coughing or wheezing? Have pains in your chest? The nurse will use a stethoscope to check your heart and lungs.

FEEL THE BEAT. When a nurse takes your pulse, he or she counts the number of times that your heart beats in a minute. Too many or too few may mean you have health problems.

In intensive care units, each nurse monitors and cares for just one or two patients. In general wards, where lives are not in danger, each nurse might have from five to eight patients to observe and care for.

PUMP IT UP. When we are well, our hearts pump blood at a steady, even pressure. But this changes when we are sick, so nurses check it carefully.

TLC (TENDER LOVING CARE)—AND MUCH MORE. In addition to observing their patients, kind, caring nurses do a great deal to calm, comfort, and encourage them. They also "speak up" for patients, communicating their needs and fears and worries, when patients are too old, young, or sick to express themselves.

WRITE IT DOWN. Records of vital signs show how sick a patient is, or how well he or she is recovering. Florence Nightingale was the first to make nurses record patient information. It is still very useful for medical staff today.

Think Clearly, Act Quickly, Keep Calm

ars, earthquakes, floods, famines, epidemics, vehicle accidents, and terrorist attacks all bring tragedy to our world. Who do we turn to for help in these disasters? Very often, it's a nurse. Along with local volunteers, nurses are usually the first on the scene in any emergency. Hundreds of lives may depend on their actions. They are highly trained professionals, and many are amazing heroes. But, even so, their work is extremely stressful and demanding. Could you do it?

DISASTER ZONE. Some nurses are specially trained to help people after natural disasters, such as major earthquakes. They must adapt to their surroundings and think on their feet.

It's not easy, but I've been trained for this!

You Can Do It!

Using a library or the Internet, look up some of the countries where nurses from the Red Cross and the Red Crescent are working, and find out how they have helped the people in those areas.

This is what we've practiced for!

LIFE SAVERS. From small beginnings in 1863, the International Red Cross and Red Crescent Movement has grown to become the largest humanitarian (caring) organization in the world. Today, it has almost 100 million staff and volunteers. They help any human in need, anywhere.

SURVIVING STRESSFUL SITUATIONS.

To cope with the pressures of being a nurse so you can successfully help others:

1. Look after yourself, as well as your patients.
2. Eat well and exercise.
3. Find time to rest and relax.
4. Speak up about any problems.
5. Share your worries and fears.
6. Get training for new or difficult tasks.
7. Practice for emergencies.
8. Learn to work well in a team.
9. Don't be afraid to ask for help or advice.
10. Find extra strength from religious beliefs or political and moral ideals.

We Have the Technology

If a nurse from long ago could travel forward in time, she'd be amazed at how hospitals have changed. Today, nurses use the latest electronics to diagnose illnesses and injuries and perform lifesaving tasks, from keeping patients' hearts beating to feeding tiny babies and delivering precise doses of powerful medicines and painkillers. Technology also monitors patients' vital signs and warns of sudden, risky changes.

Modern medical machines are wonderful, but require skill and intelligence to operate. They are only as good as the expert nurses who work with them.

WIRED UP. Hopefully you will never need to be a patient in an intensive care unit. But if you were, you would find yourself hooked up to many machines. They would help keep you alive—even breathing for you, if necessary! And they would send the nurse minute-by-minute information about you.

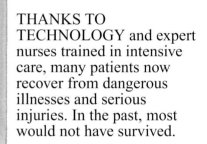
THANKS TO TECHNOLOGY and expert nurses trained in intensive care, many patients now recover from dangerous illnesses and serious injuries. In the past, most would not have survived.

23

Daring to Care

Would you dare to face death and danger, if you didn't have to? Thousands of women did during the Civil War, World War I, and World War II. They volunteered to nurse wounded soldiers, mix medicines, wash bloody uniforms, make beds, and roll bandages. They helped save lives, and their bravery won great respect and admiration. At first, volunteer war nurses were disorganized and untrained. But Florence Nightingale fought to send professional nurses to all British Army hospitals. And in 1901, the United States Army Nurse Corps was founded.

Ignore the guns – look after the patient!

Modern army nurses are trained in fitness, discipline, and combat as well as nursing skills. They have to work alongside fighting troops in very dangerous conditions.

SPECIAL SKILLS. Today's army, navy, and air force nurses are experts in emergency and critical care, operating room work, burn treatment, and plastic surgery.

NOT TOUGH ENOUGH? For centuries, army nurses were men. Officers said that women wouldn't do well in battlefield conditions. The nurse volunteers proved them wrong!

COMPASSION AND COMFORT. Mary Seacole (1805–1881) traveled from Jamaica to Britain, then to the war zone in Crimea (Russia). She set up a meeting house for wounded British soldiers, gave them food and drink to warm them up, and mixed Caribbean herbal remedies to soothe their pain.

Care in the Community

You never know when you might meet a nurse! Today, trained nurses don't just work in hospitals. They care for people in all kinds of places—at work, on vacation, in offices, factories, airports, at building sites, big shopping malls, community centers, on film sets, at sports stadiums, and more. Nurses make home visits to people too old or too sick to visit a doctor, and run drop-in centers to treat minor illnesses and injuries. They also teach classes on healthy living, gentle exercise, baby care, and first aid.

HELLO TO HEALTH. The first community nursing services began in England in 1859. Well-wishers paid for nurses to visit people in low-income neighborhoods.

This is our new product—try it!

DIFFERENT OPPORTUNITIES. Nurses also sometimes work as researchers and salespeople for pharmaceutical and cosmetics companies, or advise businesses, governments, and the media.

Be more careful in the future!

Top Tip

Learn from nurses how to stop the spread of disease. Wash your hands before eating, after sports, after feeding or cleaning pets, and after going to the bathroom.

LEARN ALL ABOUT IT.
Prevention is better than cure!
Nurses give talks to young people, teaching them how to stay healthy and answering their health questions.

MOTHERS AND BABIES.
Nurses with special training visit new mothers in their own homes, to check on the child's progress and the mother's well-being.

Nursing Past, Present, and Future

Nursing is one of the oldest careers, but it has changed a lot over the centuries. And nurses today are still learning new skills and new techniques, based on the latest medical knowledge. They work as members of health-care teams in hospitals and the community, to help save millions of lives. They also go to dangerous or disadvantaged places, to bring better health care to people living there. Whatever they do, and wherever they do it, we really wouldn't want to live without nurses!

This will soothe him!

PAST. At home or in the hospital, nurses long ago kept patients comfortable, but often could not cure them.

You're making good progress!

PRESENT. Old-style caring skills are still important for nurses and their patients. But today's nurses also have many new duties, such as monitoring their patients' vital signs using complex machines, and ordering medical tests where needed.

FUTURE. Increasingly, nurses won't just care or cure—they will also work to prevent illness from happening.

Top Tip

If you have health worries, visit the school nurse to make sure that you're doing all you can to keep yourself as healthy as possible.

SUPER-NURSES. Since 1971, highly trained nurse practitioners have taken over some of the tasks that doctors used to do. They are trained to diagnose (identify) many common diseases, and are licensed by governments to prescribe medicines to treat them.

Glossary

Amulet Lucky charm.

Anatomy Scientific study of the parts of the body.

Assess (a patient) Recognize what is wrong and decide on the best thing to do next.

Bacteria Tiny, single-celled organisms (living things) that are all around us. Some bacteria are helpful; others can cause diseases.

Commitment Being extremely devoted to a job (or a person).

Compassion Kindness, tenderness.

Competence Being skillful; doing a job well.

Diagnose Investigate a patient's symptoms and identify an illness or disease.

Hospice Peaceful, comforting care for patients who are dying; it can take place in a patient's home or in a hospice center.

Humanitarian Helping and caring for humans in need.

Infect Pass on a disease.

Inhaler Medical device that delivers a measured dose of medicine into the body through the mouth.

Instinct Inborn feelings and behavior.

Intensive care (also called **critical care**) Hospital rooms with special equipment and nursing staff to care for and monitor patients who are extremely sick.

Lice Tiny bloodsucking insects that live on humans and other animals.

Pest house In the past, a place where people with infectious diseases were locked away, so they didn't infect others.

Physiology Scientific study of how the body works.

Plastic surgery Operation to change a patient's appearance or to rebuild damaged parts of a patient's body.

Prescribe Select and give the best medicine to treat a patient's illness or relieve his or her suffering.

Professional A well-trained, respected person who is paid for his or her skills.

Quaker A member of the Society of Friends, a Christian-based religious movement that began in England in the 1650s. Quakers have worked for peace, tolerance, equality, and social justice in many parts of the world.

Remedies Medicines or other substances designed to cure disease.

Stethoscope A medical device that helps doctors and nurses investigate a patient's heart, lungs, stomach, and blood flow.

Surgery Medical treament that involves operating on and/or cutting open the body.

Symptoms Changes (such as swelling or a rash) and/or pains in the body caused by disease. Each disease has its own special symptoms, though many symptoms can be caused by a variety of diseases.

Virus A tiny organism (living thing) that grows inside the cells of humans, animals, and plants, and causes disease.

Vital signs Body functions, such as heart rate, blood pressure, and temperature, that give important information about a patient's state of health or illness.

Index

Nursing Heroes

There are a lot of nursing heroes in addition to the famous women you've just read about. Here is a list of some of them. You can do your own research to find out more.

Elizabeth Fry (1780–1845)
Inspired by her Quaker beliefs, Fry campaigned to reform prisons, help homeless people, and improve nursing care. In 1840, she set up a small nursing school in London. Later, some of her nurses worked with Florence Nightingale.

Mary Eliza Mahoney (1845–1926)
The daughter of freed slaves, Mahoney became the first African American to qualify as a trained nurse, in 1879. She was highly praised for her caring skills, and campaigned to abolish discrimination against nurses from minority communities.

Lillian Wald (1867–1940)
Wald was shocked by poverty and sickness in big cities. In 1893, in New York, she pioneered public health nursing. Wald's nurses not only cared for sick people but also offered free health checkups and advice on staying well, and worked to improve food, housing, education, and welfare services.

Mary Breckenridge (1881–1965)
Breckenridge lived in the Kentucky countryside, far from doctors and nurses. After both her children died, she vowed to help other mothers and their families. She trained as a nurse and a midwife, and then, in 1925, set up the Frontier Nursing Service. It still trains and sends nurses to remote areas today.

Mother Teresa (1910–1997)
Born in present-day Macedonia, she became a nun, and then traveled to India to care for dying people in the slums. She devoted her life to "the poorest of the poor" and recruited thousands of nurses to help her, in over 100 countries.

Hazel Johnson-Brown (1927–2011)
Brown had a brilliant career, serving as chief of the Army Nursing Corps, and then as a leader in modern nurse education. In 1979, she became the first African American woman to reach the rank of brigadier-general.

Did You Know?

In opinion polls, nurses are regularly voted the "most trusted professionals."

On average, a hospital nurse walks at least 4 miles (6.4 kilometers) every day while caring for patients.

Hospitals are not always safe places to be. For example, American nurses report over 35,000 back injuries at work (mostly from lifting or moving patients) every year.

In 2010, researchers found that, on average, nurses washed their hands around 100 times during each 10-hour shift.

Japanese engineers have built robots to take over some of the simpler nursing duties, such as washing patients and carrying them to the bathroom.

In the United States and the UK, there are around four times as many nurses as doctors.

Worldwide, about one nurse in every ten is a man.

There are more than 20 million trained nurses working today, but they are not spread equally around the globe:

• In Africa, there are 805,000 nurses; that averages out to be 11 nurses for every 10,000 people.

• In North America and South America, there are 5,259,000 nurses; that is 61 nurses for every 10,000 people.

• In Europe, there are 6,620,000 nurses; that is 75 nurses for every 10,000 people.